A Start at the Piano

By Ernest Lubin

Amsco Music Publishing Company

New York · London · Sydney

Photo credits:
Herbert Wise — technical
Iris Weinstein — pp. 17, 23, 48, 64
Mark Stein — p. 20
Herbert Wise — pp. 31, 55

Edited by Brenda Murphy
Book design by Barbara Hoffman

Order No. AM40650
ISBN 0.8256.2149.6
Library of Congress Catalog Card Number: 78-110975

Exclusive Distributors:
Music Sales Corporation
24 East 22nd Street, New York, NY 10010, USA
Music Sales Limited
78 Newman Street, London W1P 3LA, England
Music Sales Pty. Limited
27 Clarendon Street, Artarmon, Sydney, NSW 2064, Australia

Printed in the United States of America by
Port City Press
2/84

Contents

Foreword

The revised edition of *A Start at the Piano* reflects several changes. These include a brand new design (inside and out) and totally reengraved music; a complete transcription of the Bach prelude discussed in the lessons; additional pieces by Czerny and Schumann; and new selections by the great twentieth-century composer, Igor Stravinsky.

The appeal of the original book—its positive pat-on-the-back feeling and thorough step-by-step method of learning—has been carefully preserved throughout. Each new step builds on preceding ones for easy and logical progress. And, because Mr. Lubin's tone is unfailingly supportive and encouraging, the reader quickly realizes that a little effort and concentration can result in real accomplishment.

The Publishers

Preface

Not long ago I happened to call my friend, Eugene Weintraub of the Amsco Music Publishing Company about some trifling matter, and he surprised me by asking, before the conversation was over, if I'd like to write a book for him. A visit disclosed that what he had in mind was nothing less than to do for the piano what Earl Robinson has done for the guitar in his delightful book; that is, to take someone who knows nothing at all about the instrument, and to teach him enough about it—entirely on his own—to derive pleasure from it.

Mr. Robinson has succeeded brilliantly in his guitar book but the piano is obviously quite another story, and my first reaction was to doubt that it was possible. However, I said I'd try, and to my surprise the first lesson got itself written that very evening. And following Schumann's advice, who said that to compose a symphony all you need is the first bar, I found that one thing led to another and that in time all twenty lessons were completed.

While this book was conceived with the idea of helping someone to learn a little about the piano even if he had no teacher, it is of course all the better if it can be used with the help of a teacher. Naturally the teacher, or the student, if he works alone, will have to decide how much time to spend on each lesson before going on to another one. Some sections of the book require much more time than others, and each person must decide for himself what will work best for him. One thing is certain however—you can only get out of this book what you put into it. But if you have time and patience, and if you have a piano, perhaps it may open a door for you to the world of music.

Preliminaries

How many of us have dreamed of learning to play the piano, and put it off because we felt it might be too difficult. Well, it *is* difficult, particularly to play well. But it's not impossible. Certainly, it's not difficult to make a start. In fact, most of us have been near enough to a piano to make something of a start on our own, and if we had a good ear, we may have accomplished more than we realize.

While this book cannot pretend to make a pianist out of you—for that you need a teacher and some hard work—it can help you to make a start, and it can help teach you a little about the piano until you find a teacher. And perhaps it may make you a little better prepared when you do start lessons.

In the meantime, however, don't be afraid of the piano. You may do many things wrong, but you may even do some things right. Let us begin by walking to the piano and playing a note or two. Can you play chopsticks? Or can you pick up a simple tune by ear? Well, that's a beginning, and we may be able to build from there.

Let us first become acquainted with a few necessary technicalities. We will have to learn the names of the notes for one thing. And we will have to learn the names of the fingers from a pianist's point of view. That at least is very simple—they are numbered from one to five beginning with the thumb, and the little numbers above (or below) the notes in piano music show what finger you have to play the note with.

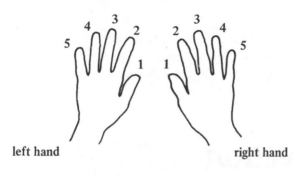

left hand   right hand

And then too we will have to learn how long to hold the notes. That's very important, too, but we shall put it off until the next chapter, since we simply can't start with everything at once.

The Keyboard

Now let us take another look at the piano. Some notes are white and some are black, and you will notice that the black notes are arranged in groups of twos and threes. It will be easier to start playing with the white notes, but we have to identify them in relation to the black notes. The white note between the two black notes is called "D," and if you count them you will see that there are seven Ds on the piano altogether.

Let us take the D nearest the middle of the piano, under the piano maker's name. That is "middle" D, and the next white note below it is middle C. Going down two more steps we find B and A, and going up from D we have E, F, and G. Then we start a new series with A again.

To return to the middle C, which we shall use as our starting point at the piano—put the thumb of your right hand on middle C and play it. And now, with your thumb resting over C, place one finger over each successive note without skipping any. This will bring you up to G. Now beginning with C, play all five notes slowly, one after another. Then play G again, and play the same notes going down. This will be our first exercise, and we shall see how it looks in music notation.

Now you have taken your first step toward becoming a pianist, but there is a good deal to think about before going further. For example, some positions of the hand are easier to work with than others, and naturally it will be a good idea to get into the habit of using a good hand position.

A Note on Hand Position

Look at the photo below. This represents a normal and correct position of the hand at the piano. You will notice that the fingers are curved and that the top of the finger plays a note by falling directly from above. This is the most important single detail to remember about your hand position, for the commonest mistake that beginners make is to play with the fingers flat.

correct hand position

Here below is a picture of what *not* to do! It's possible to play the piano like that, but it's difficult and ungainly, and you won't get very far that way.

incorrect position

One other detail is important to remember: Keep the wrist fairly low, about on a level with the keys. Thus the hand will be slightly arched, with the highest point at the knuckles. Possibly it may help at the beginning to imagine that you are holding a small object in the hollow of your hand as you play, and you can even make the experiment of stuffing a very small wad of paper into the hollow of your hand, and playing a note or two without letting it drop. This may help curve the hand. Don't try this too long, though, for it may make the hand a little tense, and you'll get the best results at the piano by being as relaxed as you can (while, of course, keeping a good hand position).

wrist even with keys

This will all take a little time and practice. Don't become discouraged if you can't attain an ideal hand position at the beginning. Just do the best you can, and keep on playing. You may find it helpful to observe the hand position of other pianists as they play. Perhaps you can get to a concert, or catch a pianist on TV, or you may have friends who play the piano well. Incidentally, there is no one precise position that applies to every hand. Each pianist tends to find his own way of playing within the framework of a normal position at the piano.

Now that we have spent a little time discussing hand position, try that exercise we did at first, but this time do it with as good a hand position as you can.

Here is the exercise again.

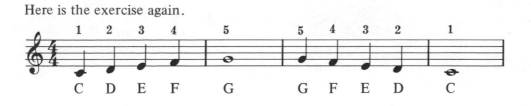

Notice, by the way, that the fingers should be directly above the keys, but not actually touching them except for the key that is being played. Another common mistake that beginners make is to let their fingers fly in the air in all directions when they are not playing a note. Here is another photo of what to avoid!

fingers too high

Of course you will have to play this exercise rather slowly if you are going to remember all the things we said about hand position, but it is good to play slowly when you are practicing. Later on it will be easy enough to play as fast as you want.

Now that you have played this exercise with the right hand, try it with the left an octave lower. That is, begin with the left hand on the first C that you come to below middle C, and start with the fifth finger.

Here is how the left hand looks in music notation.

(bass clef)

In order to write notes in the lower range, for the left hand, we need a different clef. For the right hand we have used the *treble clef* or *G clef* (𝄞), so named because it circles the line on which G above middle C is written. For the left hand we will use the *bass clef* or *F clef* (𝄢) which brackets the line on which F below middle C is written.

If you've practiced these exercises even as much as a few minutes with each hand, that's enough for now. There's a limit to how long you can practice an exercise like this without getting tired. But when you can do it fairly well, and would like something more difficult, then play both hands together an octave apart, and so evenly that they sound like one. That's more difficult than you think, but you can try it, and it will give you something to aim for as you keep practicing.

both hands together:

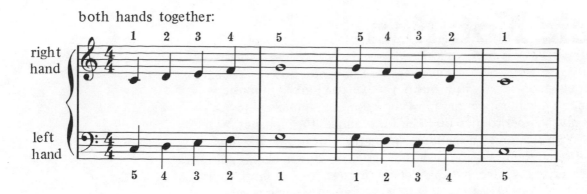

As you play this exercise, hold each note until you have sounded the next note, and then let it go. This smooth joining of notes is called *legato*, and is normally used for most of the music you play. The opposite is called *staccato*, and means that the notes are played sharply and separated from each other.

We will soon be taking up a great many new and more difficult things, but this little five-finger exercise will be useful for a long time in developing a good hand position and in acquiring facility at the piano. Keep practicing it every day for a few moments as a warming up exercise in each hand and in both hands together before you go on to anything else.

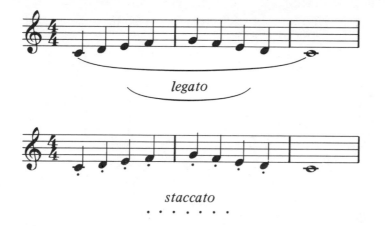

legato

staccato

Music Notation

In the first lesson we saw how our finger exercise looked in music notation, and you will notice that music notation is a simple and logical system. It's much easier to pick up than, for example, the alphabet, which we all learned easily enough as children. When the notes go up the music goes up, and when the notes go down the music goes down, and as you will observe, each successive line and space stands for a successive musical pitch.

Since we have started with middle C, let us look at it again in music notation. Here, first, is where the note is on the keyboard,

and here it is in music notation. Look at it, and then play it.

The next note going up, D, looks like this. Play this one too.

Then comes E, which looks like this. Play it.

Now let us come back to C once more, and play it again.

These four notes together, one after another, form the beginning of the familiar French folk song, "Frère Jacques," and here is how they look in music notation.

Try playing these four notes one after another very steadily and evenly. They make up a musical unit known as a *bar* or *measure*. Marking the end of the bar is a straight line called the *barline*.

If you sing "Frère Jacques" you will notice that the first bar is repeated. Try playing it twice; here is how it is written.

Going ahead with the next measure of this tune, you will see that it has only three notes, but that the last note is held twice as long as the others. Try this at the piano; here is how it looks.

To indicate that the last note is held twice as long as the others, a slightly different note is used, with its head outlined instead of being filled in. This kind of note is called a *half note* while the others are called *quarter notes*.

The easiest way of learning to play notes of different lengths correctly is to count in terms of quarter notes, holding each quarter note for one count, and each half note for two counts, while counting four beats to a measure. If we go back to "Frère Jacques" again, it will provide us with a simple illustration of how to count. Here are the first four bars of "Frère Jacques" in music notation.

Frè - re Jacqu - es,   Frè - re Jacqu - es,   dor - mez vous?   dor - mez vous?

Try playing it and singing the words, while following the music notation with your eyes at the same time.

Now do it again, but instead of singing the words, sing the counts of the measure as follows.

One...   two...   three...   four...   One...   two...   three...   four...

One...   two...   three...   four...   One...   two...   three...   four...

In the last two measures be sure to count the third and fourth beats while you hold the note G. Remember that once you start to count, you must continue to count the beats evenly without stopping. You can hold a note longer, but you can't hold a beat longer. In a way, the fundamental beat that you establish in music might be compared to the heartbeat, which keeps going steadily whether you are moving slower or faster.

Of course, the notes of the music can move faster as well as slower than the beat. The continuation of "Frère Jacques" is a good example of that, for in the next measures the first four notes move twice as fast as quarter beats. Notes of this type are called *eighth notes* and look like this.

Now here is the entire melody of "Frère Jacques" in music notation, and you will see how the eighth notes fit into the pattern of the measure.

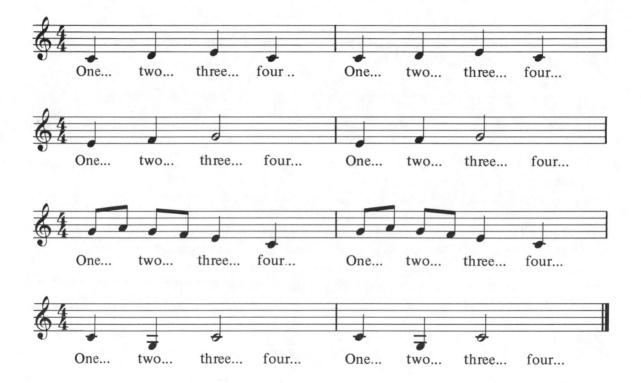

The second part of the melody is a little harder to play at the piano than the first, since the range moves beyond the five notes that we have been working with so far, and you don't have to feel that it's necessary to be able to play it at the piano just yet. If you want to try it, go ahead—but you will have to adjust the fingering. At the beginning of the fifth and seventh measures, shift your hand position by using the fingering indicated below.

America

In case you've been wondering about the two numbers ($\frac{4}{4}$) at the beginning of "Frère Jacques," that's called the *time signature*. The top number indicates that there are four beats in each measure, and the bottom number indicates that each beat is a quarter note.

Often measures can be counted in threes. Does any example come to mind? If you thought of the "Blue Danube Waltz," you're right of course, for every waltz is counted in threes. In this case, the slight accent which falls on the first beat of every measure occurs every three counts, instead of every four counts as in "Frère Jacques."

Both our national anthems, "America" and the "Star-Spangled Banner," are in three-quarter time. *

Since "America" is the simpler of the two let us try it as our first piano piece in three-quarter time. This melody has a range of only five notes in its first part which will make it relatively easy to play at the piano. However, although the music starts on middle C, the lowest note is going to be one note lower, B. Therefore let us begin on middle C with the second finger so that the thumb will be free to play B when it appears. Try it by ear and see if you can get it. Here it is in music notation.

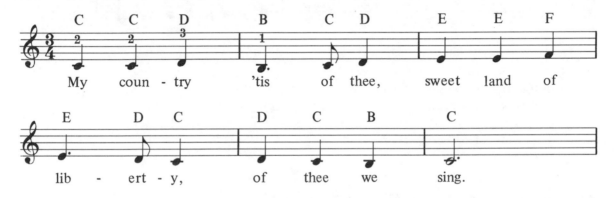

As you notice, it is in six measures of three-quarter time. There is an eighth note in the second measure, and another in the fourth measure, and since each measure has to have three full beats, we will hold the first quarter note of these measures a little longer to round out the three beats. This is indicated musically by adding a dot after these quarter notes, and you will see a dot used this way quite frequently. Technically, a dot after a note means that you extend it by half again its own length. Therefore, when you add a dot after a quarter note, it means that you have extended it by half of itself, or an eighth note; and when you add a dot after a half note, it means that you have extended it by half of itself, or in this case a quarter note. Thus a *dotted half note* is equal in counts to a half plus a quarter note, or three quarter notes. The last measure of our phrase of "America" is a dotted half note, which must be counted for three beats.

---

*You might like to notice an interesting difference rhythmically between these two anthems—although they are both in $\frac{3}{4}$ time, "America" starts on the first beat of the measure while "The Star-Spangled Banner" begins with an upbeat, that is, on a weak beat before the beginning of the first full measure. If you sing them with the words, the difference will become clear. "*My* country, *'tis* of thee" obviously starts on a strong beat, while "Oh, *say* can you *see*" begins with a weak beat that leads into the strong beat on "say." Musical compositions are about equally divided into those that start with a downbeat and those that start with an upbeat, and it is a good way of testing your ear and your sense of rhythm to see if you can tell the difference as you listen to a piece of music. There is a very close analogy to poetical metre, where "dactylic" lines start with a downbeat, and "iambic" lines start with an upbeat.

Now try playing "America" while counting, out loud, the three quarter beats in the measure. It's a little tricky due to the dotted quarter notes in measures two and four—they are held while you count one and two, and the eighth note comes in just before you count three. But if you count evenly and steadily and play the tune correctly in time, you may be able to get it. Here it is again in music notation, with the counts written in where they occur.

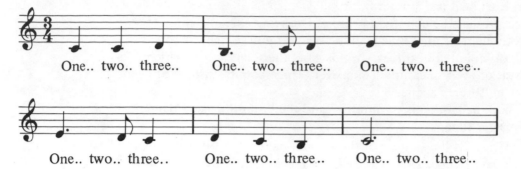

One.. two.. three..   One.. two.. three..   One.. two.. three..

One.. two.. three..   One.. two.. three..   One.. two.. three..

The second, fourth, and sixth measures of the piece could also have been written as follows.

The little curved line underneath the second and fourth and sixth measures is called a *tie*, and it means that you hold the second of the two connected notes without playing it again. Very likely the notation might be clearer that way, but the abbreviation of a dot after a note to indicate its being held for an extra half of its own length is used wherever possible, and we might as well get to know it!

Suggestions for Practice

At this stage you can hardly practice very long at a time—even ten or fifteen minutes is quite enough to spend on the material we have had so far. But do get into the habit of practicing consistently every single day. If you really want to learn to play the piano, this is the only way you can do it!

Begin each practice session with the five-finger exercise we had in the beginning. Work on it slowly and carefully and watch your hand position. Do it with each hand separately first, and then try it with hands together a little more slowly. Later on you can vary it occasionally by speeding it up a little, while still being careful to keep a good hand position.

Then work a little each day on the new piece of this lesson, "America," until you can get to play it quite easily and naturally.

Don't forget to give some time at each practice session to reviewing your old pieces. So far we only have one old piece that we can review, "Frère Jacques," but go over it as conscientiously as your new piece. The fifth and sixth measures of "Frère Jacques" are the most difficult, so practice them by themselves sometimes until they come to you as easily as the rest of the piece.

A Little Extra Practice

By now we have covered quite a good bit of ground, and before taking up anything new it might be helpful to apply what we have already learned to some other melodies.

Since we began with "Frère Jacques," here is another very charming French folksong, the first part of which is within the range of a few notes and uses simple rhythms.

Can you recognize it from looking at the music? If not, it is "Au Clair de la Lune," which you very likely know. This piece is in four-quarter time and begins with the thumb on middle C. As you notice, the first measure consists of four quarter notes, while the second measure has only two half notes. But since each half note is counted for two beats, these two notes are equivalent in time to the four quarter notes. The third measure is made up of four quarter notes again, while the last measure has one long note of four beats, which fills up the entire measure. This kind of note is called a *whole note* (o).

Play it again, counting the beats out loud. This is always good practice for learning to play in time.

Notice that these four bars are repeated. That is what the double bar with two dots at the end of the last measure indicates. It is called a *repeat sign*, and is often used to save space.

Would you like to play the next section of "Au Clair de la Lune"? Luckily, it has a range of only five notes, but since the notes are lower, going down to G below middle C, we will have to change the position of our hand and start this phrase on D with the fifth finger. Here it is in music notation.

If you prefer you can play these same notes with the left hand beginning with the thumb. Here is how it looks written in the bass clef for the left hand.

After you have played this middle section, go back to the first part and play it again to finish the piece.

Now here is another melody that we should be able to work out using the knowledge we have acquired.

Start this one with the third finger on E.

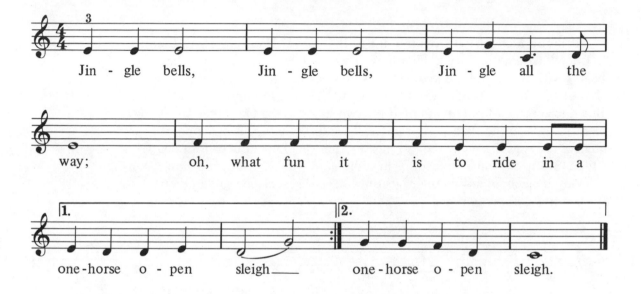

This piece, as you notice, also has a repeat sign at the end, and the lines above the music with the numbers 1 and 2 underneath them mean that the two bars under figure 1 are played the first time around, and on the repeat you omit them and go directly to the two bars under figure 2.

This melody is somewhat more complicated rhythmically than "Au Clair de la Lune," but since it only uses the material we have taken up so far, you should be able to learn it with a little practice. Of course, it's the familiar refrain of "Jingle Bells," and you can probably play it by ear in case you have trouble reading the music. But in this case, go back to the printed music, and follow it with your eyes as you play it. This will help you familiarize yourself with music notation.

If later on you want to play this piece faster, go ahead and do so. You can count the beats at any speed you want, as long as you count them steadily once you establish the speed, or *tempo*.

Suggestions for Practice

By now you have a few different pieces to play. Keep them all in practice, concentrating on one or another of them on different days. After you have learned them all, go through your entire repertoire in order sometimes.

Don't forget to keep practicing the five-finger exercises at the beginning of each practice session. They will help you to limber up your fingers, and to establish a good hand position.

If you would like some extra practice in learning music notation, pick up Howard Hanet's book, *Learn to Read Music* (Simon and Schuster). It has some excellent exercises in learning to read notes, and will give you an opportunity to practice in greater depth.

Sight Reading

Since it is so important to be able to read music, let us try a little practice now in reading notes, purely as an exercise in sight reading. These exercises are now not based on familiar melodies, since that may become something of a crutch to lean on, and we must learn to get along without it.

Here, then, are some new melodies that fall within the range of a five-finger position. Start the first one with the thumb on middle C.

At first it may be easier to learn a new melody like this by figuring out the notes first, and saving the rhythmical problems until later. If you wish, you may write the notes in letters below the musical notes, as we have done with the first two measures, but this of course is another crutch that you will learn to discard before long. After you are acquainted with the notes, do it in correct time, remembering to count the half notes for two counts, always counting the beats evenly.

Try this rhythmical variation of the first two measures, as always counting very steadily while you play.

Here is still another rhythmical variation of the first two measures. This particular rhythmic pattern occurs less frequently, but it is good practice too.

Eventually it will become second nature to distinguish between quarter notes, half notes, and dotted half notes, and later you will be able to dispense with counting out loud. But right now it is a good idea to bend over backwards to be correct rhythmically, since good rhythm is a basic requirement of good musicianship. If you have any doubts at all about the rhythm, count out loud! You can even tap your foot in time to the beat if you'd like—anything that will help you keep in time is worth doing!

Now let us practice a little in three-quarter time. In the next study all the notes are quarters except for the two dotted half notes, which are held for three counts. Again, learn the notes first, and then count it very steadily in threes.

Here are a few more exercises for rhythm. The first is entirely on middle C.

The next is in three-quarter time and is not difficult, but continue to count out loud as you play it, once you have learned the notes. Start this one with the fifth finger on G.

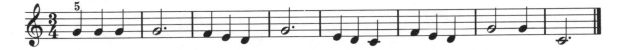

Would you like to try a little creative work yourself? If so, finish the next two melodies on your own, adding the missing four bars at the end of each piece.

The first one is in two-quarter time, which has only two beats to a measure, so you will need very few notes to complete the eight bars.

Now try one in three-quarter time.

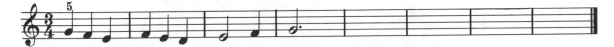

As you will discover, it is really not too difficult to invent melodies. Don't just play them at the piano, however; write them out too.

Suggestions for Practice

Now that you are learning to read notes, it is important to get all the practice you can in sight reading. If you have any other beginner's book at home, look over the first pieces in it, and see how well you can read them. Feel free at this stage to write in the letters of the notes above the music, if you find it helpful.

An excellent beginner's book for supplementary practice is the *Book for Older Beginners* by John Thompson (Willis Music Co.). Get it, if possible, to add to the work you are doing in this book. The pieces on the first few pages are excellent material for practice.

Another book with a wealth of valuable material for practice in sight reading is Denes Agay's *The Young Pianist's First Book* (Warner Bros. Music). Get this too if you can, and see how well you can do with the early pieces in it.

Always remember that the rhythm is just as important as the notes. Often it is a good idea to practice the rhythmical patterns by themselves. You can tap your foot in time to the beats as you count them out loud, while clapping the rhythmical pattern, or playing it on one note. When you are sure of the rhythm, then apply it to the notes of the piece.

Of course, writing your own music is an excellent way of practicing the notes. In case you do the creative exercises in this lesson, then carefully write out what you have composed and practice your own music along with the other pieces you are learning.

Chords

While most of the melodies we have had so far mainly move stepwise—that is, from one note to its neighboring one—there are also many melodies that are based on skips. The beginning of "The Star-Spangled Banner" is a typical example.

If you take the three notes of the first full measure, C, E, and G, and play them at the same time, you will find that they sound quite well together.

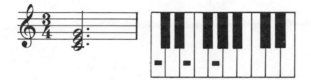

This happens to be one of the most commonly used chords in music, and if you want to be technical about it, you can call it the *tonic chord, or* the I (one) chord in C, or the *C Major chord.*

The notes of this chord often turn up in other melodies. Here's another example in "Sweet Betsy from Pike."

As you can see, the notes of the first measure again make up the C Major chord. If you try playing the three notes of the second measure together (G, F, and D), you will find that they too form a chord.

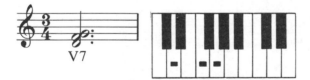

This is also a very commonly used chord; it is one of the positions of the *dominant seventh chord*, or the *five seven chord* (written V^7).

These two chords, the I and V⁷ are so important and so useful that you
will find it well worth the trouble of getting to know them. Play them a few
times, one after another, in the right hand.

And now, to become even more familiar with them, try playing them in
the left hand an octave lower (that is, start with the C, E, and G below middle C).

Now, try these chords in both hands together. (This may not be too easy
at first, but you'll get it with a little practice.)

With these two chords alone it is now possible to harmonize a great
many melodies. Since we usually play the melody in the right hand and the
accompaniment in the left, review the chords once more in the left hand,
and then we will put a melody on top of them.

Can you still play the melody of "America" that we had in the last lesson? Review it in the right hand, and then try playing it together with the I
and the V⁷ chords as follows.

The rest of "America" can be harmonized with these two chords.

However, it does not fit ideally; the measure before the last is quite frankly a makeshift. We will have to learn a number of new chords, as well as new positions of the I and V^7 chords before we can harmonize melodies just as we might wish. At this stage we are something like a person who knows pidgin English—our abilities are rather limited, but at least we can get along a little.

A Few Simple Pieces

Now that we know two chords, let us see if we can make up a few simple pieces based on them. Perhaps you may even find that you can invent melodies yourself to go along with them. Here is one possibility.

Notice the tie connecting the right-hand notes in the last two measures. That means you hold them continuously for their combined length, or six counts in all, while repeating the left-hand chords which are not tied.

Here is another melody based on our two chords. It is a little more difficult than the first because its range is seven notes instead of five, and that will mean adjusting the fingering to include the notes below middle C that occur in the second and seventh measures. But you may find you can handle it if you practice the melody alone at first. Start by learning the notes, and writing them in above the staff yourself if you find that helpful. After you have learned the notes, play them in correct time, counting out loud if necessary.

That little crossed note at the beginning of the seventh measure is called a *grace note* (♪), and it means that you can play it in your own time before the regular note which it precedes, making it as short as you wish.

Arpeggios

Chords in the left hand can be varied by playing them as *arpeggios*, one note after another instead of all together.

Here is another miniature piece based on these two chords, this time used in arpeggio form.

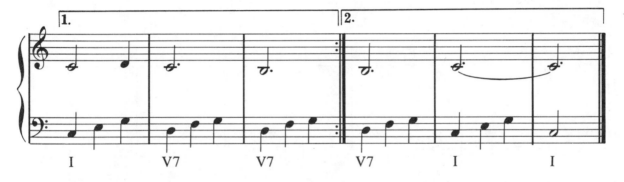

Here again you may find it a good idea to work a little on each hand before putting them together. Don't forget to observe the repeat sign with the first and second endings. The first time play it directly to the double bar repeat sign, and on the repetition, skip the three bars under figure 1, and go right on to the second ending under figure 2.

Rests

Now if you have learned the little piece, let us try a variation of it. Instead of adding notes, we shall leave out a few. Just as we learned to count notes for a certain number of beats, we must now learn to count *rests* which indicate that no note at all is to be sounded. A quarter rest looks like this (𝄽) and indicates silence for one beat; and as for the others, see the table.

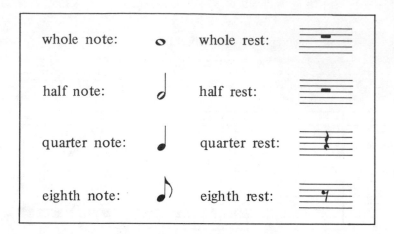

whole note:	𝅝	whole rest:	▬
half note:	𝅗𝅥	half rest:	▬
quarter note:	♩	quarter rest:	𝄽
eighth note:	♪	eighth rest:	𝄾

Now let us vary the left hand of our piece by taking out some of the notes and substituting rests—see if you can learn to play it this way.

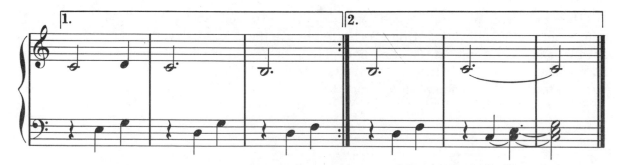

If you find the left hand a bit difficult, practice it by itself until you get it, then add the right hand.

Do you prefer this version of the piece? It will be easier for the melody in the right hand to come through since there is no accompaniment on the first beat of each measure; as you gradually become a better pianist you will notice that your pieces sound better when you can make the melody sing out above the accompaniment. As you listen to recordings of great pianists, it is interesting to notice this point as a detail in their artistry. In your own playing, this is one of the things that you keep in mind to master; if you don't find it easy right now, be patient.

Would you like to try still one more variation of this little piece? Play the whole thing an octave higher, both the right hand and the left. (Perhaps you know now what an *octave* is—it is the distance of eight notes after which the same notes are repeated at a different level, either higher or lower.)

Here is how our piece looks at the higher octave. Now we will have to write both hands in the G clef (or *treble clef*), for the left hand will be moving up from middle C, and it would take too many leger lines to indicate it in the *bass clef* (𝄢). Of course, the right hand will now be in the higher register, and it is not easy to read it up there. But as long as you have learned it at the lower octave, it won't be difficult to just take it up an octave.

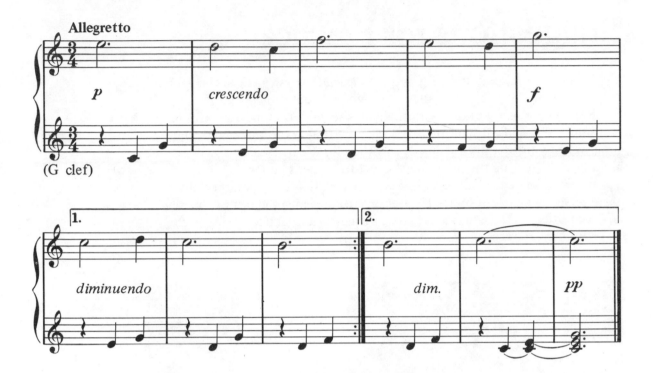

Perhaps you may prefer this version to the original one at the lower octave. Learn it as well as you can, and see if you can memorize it. With a little practice you may find that you can play it without having to look at the music anymore.

By the way, notice a few new indications that we have added. The tempo direction at the very beginning, *allegretto*, means moderately fast, *crescendo* means get louder, and *diminuendo* means get softer. *Crescendo* is often abbreviated *cresc.*, and *diminuendo, dim.*—and even more often these directions are indicated by the symbols, ⏴══ and ══⏵

Some Performance Directions	
Allegro	fast
Allegretto	moderately fast
Moderato.	moderate speed
Andante	rather slow
Adagio.	very slow
f or forte	loud
ff or fortissimo	very loud
p or piano.	soft
pp or pianissimo	very soft

As for the letters p, f, and pp, they are abbreviations of the Italian words *piano, forte,* and *pianissimo,* meaning soft, loud, and very soft.

The direction *ritardando* at the end means that you can slow down the speed or tempo a little. Sometimes pianists do this at the end of a piece even when it's not indicated in the music. In certain cases this may be an inexcusable liberty, while in others it may be entirely appropriate. There is a very large area in the performance of any music that just has to be left to the discretion of the performer. As you continue to develop as a pianist, your own musical taste will continue to mature.

Suggestions for Practice

It may take a good deal of practice to learn the new piece in this lesson to your satisfaction—but be patient, and you will get it little by little.

Remember that working with the hands separately is most helpful in learning a new and difficult piece, so take the time to do this at the beginning. When you first put the hands together, do it particularly slowly at first, later increasing the tempo as you get to know it better.

It may also be helpful to isolate any passage that gives you special trouble, and practice it by itself, later on fitting it into the rest of the piece.

And of course, as always, be sure to begin each practice session with your five-finger exercises, and review some of your old pieces every day.

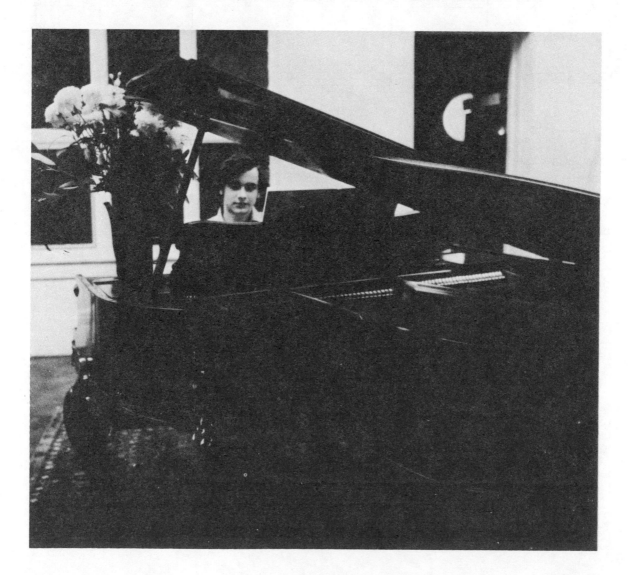

A Little Technical Work

By now we have covered a great deal of ground, and soon we shall go on to new things, such as playing melodies that go beyond the range of a five-finger hand position. But before we do, it might be a good idea to pause for breath and take time out to practice some exercises.

In our first lesson we had a very simple five-finger exercise in five notes from C to G in quarter notes, and there is no reason why you can't do this exercise every day. With all the work we've had by now, though, you may be able to do it a little faster, so let us try it now in eighth notes instead of quarter notes.

And don't forget the left hand too, an octave lower.

And of course you can try it with both hands.

If you'd like to vary this exercise, limit the number of notes to three, which will give you the opportunity of playing it with different sets of fingers.

Now we have a three-finger exercise. If you have tried it with the first, second, and third fingers you will have found that it is not at all difficult. Try it now with the second, third, and fourth fingers.

This is a little harder, but now see if you can do it with the weakest fingers of all, the third, fourth, and fifth.

This actually is quite difficult, and you had better practice it slowly at first. But these fingers always need strengthening, so the more practice you can give it, the better. Do it very slowly and strongly and firmly, almost exaggerating the finger action.

Let us try these exercises with the left hand too. You might start by varying our five-finger exercise to start with the thumb on middle C, going down to F as follows.

Now try the little three-finger exercise, beginning on middle C and going down to A, and again do it with the three possible sets of fingering that we have used in the right hand, the first, second, and third; the second, third, and fourth; and finally the most difficult, the third, fourth, and fifth.

These exercises, quite frankly, are not too interesting musically; but for the pianist they are exactly what the punching bag is for the boxer, or the exercises at the barre for the dancer, a necessary and inevitable discipline that is required in order to advance to higher levels. So be patient and spend at least a few minutes of your time at the piano warming up with these exercises—not all of them at one time, of course, but as much as you think you can profit from.

Don't forget that playing the piano, after all, is a physical activity which will only be mastered if you give it the necessary time and work. With these exercises, you will have the satisfaction of knowing that eventually they will make it possible for you to do wonderful things at the piano. This book, after all, is only a two-dimensional outline—you have to add the third dimension of time and practice to make it come to life.

The beneficial use of five fingers, five notes, was not above engaging the attention of Igor Stravinsky, the great composer. He wrote the piece "Seven Pieces on Five Notes." Should you be interested in following the thoughts of a great musical mind as he composes his five notes, turn to the Musical Supplement where we have reprinted two of the pieces, *Andantino* and *Lento*.

Suggestions for Practice

Now at last we can vary our technical exercise from the simple five-finger patterns that we learned at the beginning. However, you don't have to do everything in this lesson every single day. Use your own judgment in choosing some part of it for each practice session.

Continue to go over your old pieces, and keep up as many of them as you can.

Scales

So far, we have confined ourselves to melodies that can be played by the five fingers in a fixed position, occasionally with a slight extension for an extra note or two. But this simple approach will not serve for everything as we advance beyond this rather limited range.

If, for example, you play a complete *scale*—going up step by step from middle C to C an octave higher—you will find that you run into trouble.

Of course it would be very easy to divide the scale between the hands as follows.

But what if the left hand is busy with an accompaniment, and you want to play this scale with the right hand alone?

Fortunately there is a little trick that makes it possible, and that you will find immensely useful as you go on to do more difficult things. It is called "putting the thumb under," and if you try it you will find that it is not at all difficult.

Start by playing the first three notes of the scale—C, D, and E, with the first, second, and third fingers of the right hand—and while you keep holding the third finger down on E, shift the thumb from its original position on C to the note F above your third finger. Now you're ready to continue all the way up to high C without any further trouble.

Here is the scale on C, written with this fingering.

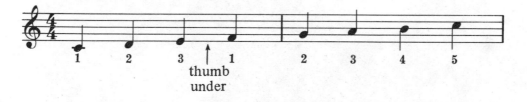

The trick of putting the thumb under is so important that it will be worth taking the time to do a few extra finger exercises to accustom ourselves to this technique.

For a moment review the three-finger exercise that we had in the last lesson.

Now substitute the thumb for the third finger on E by putting it under the hand as we have just learned to do. Here is the new fingering for this exercise.

That's not very difficult, as you see.

Now extend it a step, and make it an exercise of four notes, going from C to F. In this case, we will play E with the third finger, and cross the thumb under it at this point to play the note F. Here is the new version of the exercise.

To make this exercise work more easily, get into the habit of moving the thumb to its new position just as soon as you can after you finish playing middle C. Now with a little practice on our new exercise, you will find it much easier to go back to our scale on C with the correct fingering of crossing the thumb under. Do it a few times in succession for practice, and finish with an octave skip from middle C to high C.

Now that you have arrived at high C, you will find that it is easy to come down the scale by a process called "crossing the hand over." Play the scale going down from high C until you reach F with your thumb. Then, while holding the thumb on F, cross the hand over the thumb so that you can play the E below with the third finger. This will carry you down to D with the second finger, and C with the thumb to complete the descending scale.

Here, then, is the scale going down, with the correct fingering.

If you find you can do that without too much difficulty, then make a little exercise by going up and down the scale a few times in succession as follows.

As with all your exercises, this will benefit you the most if you play it strongly and firmly, keeping a very good hand position.

Now before going ahead any further with the right hand, we must apply what we know to the left hand too. Start on middle C with the thumb and go down to A with the third finger. Then, while holding A, put the thumb under to play G, and finish the scale down to low C as follows.

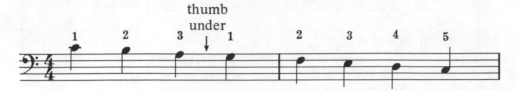

Just as we did with the right hand, let us try the exercises for putting the thumb under, first with three notes, and then with four.

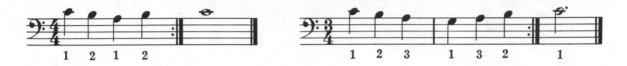

Play the entire scale of C, going down an octave, a few times, and finish with the octave skip from middle C to low C.

And now, just as we did with the right hand, reverse the scale. Start with low C this time, and go up an octave by "crossing the hand over" when you get to the thumb on G. Finish with the third finger on A, the second finger on B, and the thumb on middle C, as follows.

Finally, play the scale going up and then down a few times in succession.

If you'd like to play the scales with the hands together an octave apart, you may find it a little difficult just now, since the hands reverse themselves as far as fingering is concerned, and this makes for a little problem in coordination. But you certainly won't have any difficulty if you play the hands going in opposite directions. Start both hands with the thumbs on middle C, and then play the right hand an octave up and the left hand an octave down, and then return to middle C. You will have the same fingering in both hands, so you can save time by practicing both hands at once.

34

If you want to vary this, you can move the right hand up an octave, or the left hand down an octave, thus avoiding a collision on middle C. As usual, practice strongly and firmly, with a very good hand position. There are a few dissonances when you play the scales in opposite directions, and your neighbors may not like it, but it will help make a pianist out of you.

Suggestions for Practice

Scales form one of the most valuable additions to the technical exercises with which you begin each practice session—make the best use of them. The trick of putting the thumb under is a necessary technical tool for advancing to more difficult things, so practice it patiently and assiduously!

Continue to review your old pieces. If you have the Thompson book, you can go ahead with it on your own. Use your judgment as to how far you can go, and how much new material you can profitably take. As a general rule, it is better to do less, but to do it well.

Minor Scales

Now that we have spent a little time on scales from a technical point of view, let us turn to something more interesting and consider them from a musical point of view. The scale you have played from C to the C an octave higher using only the white notes is called the *C Major scale*—but if you were to start a white-note scale on any other note, say D or E, it would sound quite different.

To understand why, we must learn about *whole tones* and *half tones*. Play middle C again, and go up the scale to the C above, but this time play every single note between them in order, including the black notes as well as the white notes. You have just played the *chromatic scale*; there are twelve notes in it altogether until you reach the high C.

In the chromatic scale, the distance from any note to its nearest neighbor, black or white, is called a *half tone*. Thus the distance from C to D, or from D to E, which includes a black note between them, is a *whole tone*. The distance from E to F, however, is only a *half tone*, since there is no black note between them. In the scale of C Major, the only other half tone, apart from the interval between E and F, occurs between the last two notes, B and C. Thus in the C Major scale, and in every other major scale, the half tones will occur only between the *third* and *fourth* notes of the scale, and between the *seventh* and *eighth* notes of the scale.

If you wanted to play an identical major scale beginning on any other note except C it would be necessary to use one or more black notes so as to make the half tones come out between the third and fourth and between the seventh and eighth notes of the scale. Try it on D, for example. Now you will find that the third and seventh notes of the scale will have to be not the white notes F and C respectively, but the black notes just above them.

If, however, you play a scale beginning on D and use only the white notes, you will get a different arrangement of whole tones and half tones. This time the half tones occur between the second and third and between the sixth and seventh tones of the scale. You might like to play all the possible scales on the white notes, beginning with a different note each time, just to hear how they sound. There are seven altogether, and each of them has a quality of its own. These varying forms of the scale are known as *modes*, and are identified by their Greek names. The white-note scale beginning on D, for example, is called the Dorian mode, the white-note scale beginning on E, the Phrygian mode.

THE MODES

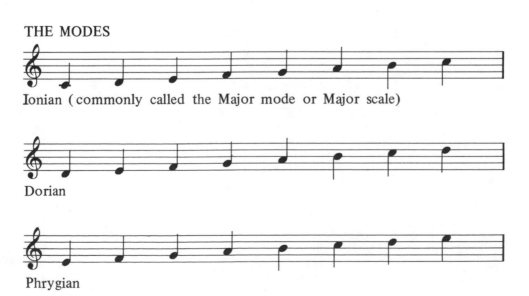

Ionian (commonly called the Major mode or Major scale)

Dorian

Phrygian

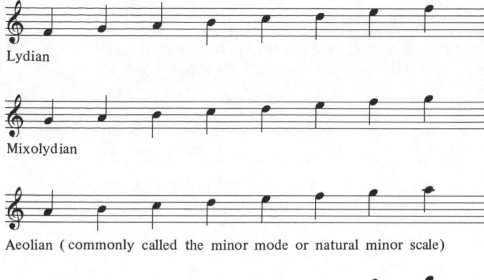

Lydian

Mixolydian

Aeolian (commonly called the minor mode or natural minor scale)

Locrian

Of all the modes, there is only one other (apart from the major scale) beginning on C that is in general use in our Western music. That is the white-note scale beginning on A, which we call the *minor scale.* Almost everything we sing or play is in either the major or the minor mode, and musical compositions are very frequently referred to by their scale, or key, as for example Beethoven's First Symphony in C Major, or Schumann's Piano Concerto in A minor.*

So far, everything we have studied has been in the key of C Major, but now let us try something in the key of A minor.

First let us play the scale of A minor, beginning on the A below middle C, and going up and then down an octave, as follows.

How do you like the sound of the minor mode? It has quite a different quality from the major mode, and some people have found it sad and plaintive. But that of course is a subjective reaction, and you may not happen to find it so at all.

*The other modes are sometimes found in folk music, and in compositions based on folk music, such as Ralph Vaughan-Williams' delightful suite on English folk songs. A beautiful and interesting use of the Lydian mode, or the white-note scale beginning on F, occurs in one of Beethoven's last quartets, that in A minor, Opus 132, which contains a section called "Song of thanks of a convalescent, in the Lydian mode."

Here is a melody in the key of A minor, beginning on low A below middle C, and opening with the first five notes of the scale. Start with the thumb on low A, and then put the thumb under when you come to D, since the range of this melody is an entire octave, and we will need this fingering to finish the piece.

Do you recognize this melody? It is the national anthem of Israel and is called "Hatikvah." With slight variations it exists as a folk song in different countries, and it is as a Bohemian folk song that Bedrich Smetana has used it in his symphonic poem, *The Moldau.*

If you have been careful to use the correct fingering you shouldn't have too much trouble learning this little melody. And now if you know it, let us accompany it with some chords in the key of A minor.

Here is the I chord in A minor. Play it in arpeggio form twice, and then in chord form twice, starting on A below middle C.

And here is the V^7 chord, beginning on B below middle C. practice it the same way, first as an arpeggio, then as a chord.

And now, just one new chord in A minor before we harmonize our melody. Although the I and V^7 chords are extremely useful, they will not harmonize everything, and we will need a different chord in the third measure, the IV chord. Practice this chord too in arpeggio form and then in chord form as follows.

Combine the new IV chord in A minor with the I and V^7 chords in this order, and make a little exercise of this series by playing it over a few times.

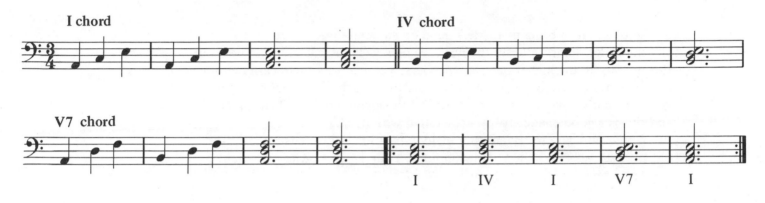

Before harmonizing our melody, we had better practice these chords in the left hand an octave lower. Try them one at a time first, and when you know them, put them together in the little series we just did in the right hand.

I chord   **IV chord**

V7 chord

Play the melody and chords together; the melody in the right hand and the chords in the left as follows.

You may vary the left-hand chords slightly in the last four measures by omitting in each chord those notes that occur in the melody in the right hand at the higher octave. Perhaps you may find that you like the harmonization better that way.

Actually the range of this melody brings the chords in the left hand rather low, and you may prefer to play the entire piece an octave higher in both hands.

Here it is in the higher range. This time we shall tie the first two chords in the left hand, and add a few expressive marks.

Notice that in bringing the left hand up an octave we have used the G clef in the left hand. And by the way, see how well you can read the notes of this melody in the higher octave. Of course you can play them easily enough in the higher octave once you have learned them in the lower octave.) You will eventually have to get used to reading the higher portion of the G clef, and this is a good chance to get acquainted with it.

Would you care to try another melody in A minor? Here is a beautiful old English folksong called "How Should I Your Truelove Know" which is sung to one of Ophelia's rhymes in *Hamlet*.

And here is another melody in A minor, a hauntingly lovely old Flemish folk song that dates from the sixteenth century. Curiously enough, the opening notes form a descending scale in C Major, beginning with an upbeat so that you really can't tell it's in A minor until you come to the end, when the minor key is unmistakable.

Play it quite slowly, and when you have learned it, follow all the expressive marks such as *piano, mezzoforte,* and *pianissimo* (i.e., *p, mf*, and *pp*, or soft, moderately loud, and extremely soft). And don't forget the *crescendo* and *diminuendo* signs, and the *ritardando* at the end.

Suggestions for Practice

Now you can begin to spend more time on your practice sessions—a half hour a day should not be too much, if you have time and perseverance.

Continue to start each practice session with a little technical work, choosing from the material we've had so far. You can also take the chords of this lesson and practice them in arpeggio form as follows; they make excellent technical practice.

By the way, two bars of three-eighth time are often combined to form one larger bar of six-eighth time, so that this exercise might also be written as follows.

Give yourself as much time as you need for this chapter. In order to learn the three pieces given in this lesson, it may very well require a longer period of time than you needed for the earlier lessons.

The Black Notes

Up to this point we have been playing exclusively on the white notes, and it's about time we gave a little attention to the black notes. In a way they are easier to play than the white notes, for they stand out from the keyboard, and there are many children who learn to play the piano by themselves starting with the black notes.

The only difficulty about the black notes is that their notation is more complicated than that of the white notes. Instead of having a letter to themselves like the white notes, they are indicated by altering the nearest white note with a special symbol, either a *sharp* (♯) or a *flat* (♭).

A sharp printed before a note means that you play the black note just *above* it, while a flat before a note means that you play the black note just *below* it. Thus, as you will notice, all the black notes can be indicated in two ways, either by sharps or by flats. Here, for example, are the two possible ways of writing the five black notes between middle C and the C above.

These two lines are read by playing exactly the same notes.

When the black notes are played beginning with F-sharp they make a kind of musical scale. It is known as the *pentatonic scale,* and is frequently found in the music of non-western peoples. If you try to invent melodies using only the black notes, you will find that they are likely to have a Chinese flavor. There is a charming piece in Maurice Ravel's *Mother Goose* suite for piano duet called "Pagodas" that is made up almost entirely of the black notes, and that delightfully conveys the oriental atmosphere Ravel desired.

Here is a little tune using the five black notes beginning on F-sharp. Start by putting the five fingers over the first five notes of the piece, which make up the five notes of the pentatonic scale.

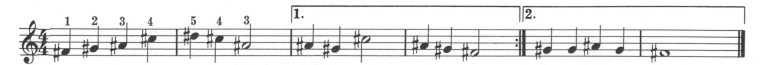

Notice that in the fifth measure only the first G is sharped. Once you have placed a sharp or flat before any note in a measure, that same note will remain a sharp or flat until the end of the measure. The only way you can cancel it is to place a *natural* sign (♮) before it.

You will occasionally find folksongs from European countries, Scotland in particular, that are built on the pentatonic scale. "The Campbells are Coming" is a good example. It will make a wonderful exercise for stretching your hand if you begin it with the thumb on the opening note, C-sharp, and use the fingering given. Most hands can stretch an octave without too much difficulty, but now you will have to reach from C-sharp to the D-sharp an octave and a note above. See what you can do with it.

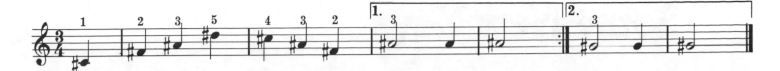

Of course you could play this melody on the white notes too. If you'd like to try it, play middle C as the first note, and just pretend the sharps aren't there. It doesn't seem to fall quite so easily under the fingers that way though.

Actually the black notes are very easy to play, and a few black notes along with the white notes are best suited to most hand positions. We shall start using them frequently now, and before long you will find yourself very much at home with them.

Suggestions for Practice

Now that we have taken up something entirely new, give yourself plenty of time for it before going ahead; as with the preceding lesson you can allow yourself considerably more time than you may have needed for the earlier lessons.

Perhaps you may be able to play other pentatonic tunes by ear on the black notes. Do you happen to know "Ye Banks and Braes o' Bonnie Doon," which is a lovely old Scottish folksong? Perhaps you can also pick up the first section of "Oh Susannah." This tune doesn't sound particularly pentatonic, but the whole first section can be play entirely on the black keys, beginning on F-sharp. The middle section introduces only one white note—can you figure out what it is?

If you can get these tunes by ear, it would be good practice to see if you can put them on music paper. Actually it is not too hard to write the notes you have played, but you may find it a little harder to write exact rhythm. Just write the notes first if you can, even without barlines if necessary, and then see if you can work out the rhythm. As a hint, "Ye Banks and Braes" is in three-quarter time, and "Oh Susannah" can be written in either two-quarter or four-quarter time. (As an extra hint, they both start with *upbeats*.)

Sometimes the main difficulty in notating music yourself is to find the beginning of each measure. You have to listen carefully to see where the slight accent of the *downbeat* occurs, and start your measure at that point.

In case you have trouble working out the rhythm of "Oh Susannah," here is the rhythm of the first bar, just to get you started.

Another good practice in notation is to rewrite the melodies which have sharps, using flats instead. That means, for example, that an F-sharp becomes a G-flat. Here is the first bar of the melody on page 42 in flats.

See if you can do the rest yourself. And write out "The Campbells Are Coming" with flats too.

Some New Keys

A couple of chapters back we noticed that you could build a major scale on D if you used two sharps, F-sharp and C-sharp. Try playing the D Major scale again—here is how it is written.

If you were to play any of your old pieces in D Major (you learned them all in C Major, of course) you would find now that these two sharps are used constantly as part of the scale and the chords. To save ourselves the trouble of writing in the sharps for F and C wherever they occur, we will simply write them both at the beginning of the line, and this means that any time an F or a C occurs in the music, it will automatically be an F-sharp or a C-sharp. Here is the scale of D with its two sharps written at the beginning.

The group of sharps or flats written at the beginning of any line of music (unless it is in the keys of C Major or A minor, which have no sharps or flats) is called a *key signature,* and you will notice that it comes just before the time signature. Although the time signature is written just once at the beginning of any piece the key signature is included at the beginning of every line of music.

Why don't you see if you can play one of your old pieces in the key of D instead of the key of C. Here is "Frère Jacques" for example, as it would be played in the key of D. You can harmonize this little melody with the I chord in D throughout.

Don't forget that every F is now F-sharp, since it is in the key of D Major now. All the Cs are C-sharps too, of course, but there just don't happen to be any in this melody.

If we go up to the next white note, E, and build a major scale on it, we will find now that it has four sharps, F, G, C, and D, as follows.

Or written with the time signature at the beginning as it customarily is:

This may seem like a difficult key at first glance, but actually it's easier to play in a key with some sharps or flats than it is in C Major, because in a way, the black notes can help you find your place among the white notes.

Frederick Chopin is said to have given his pupils this very scale of E Major as their first to practice, and if you try it you will find that it is one of the easiest to play. The fingers just naturally fall into place on the black notes, and you will see that it is less trouble putting the thumb under from G-sharp to A than it is on two white notes.

Of course you can build a minor scale as well as a major scale on any of the twelve notes of the chromatic scale. The only difference is that in the minor scale the third, sixth, and seventh notes will be a half tone *lower* than the corresponding notes of the major scale built on the same note. Thus when you write the key signature for the minor scales, they will have three flats more or three sharps less than their major ones.

For example, here is the scale of C minor.

Here is D minor.

And here is E minor.

It is interesting to note that the minor scale is treated with much greater freedom than the major scale, for there are three different forms of the minor scale in common use. The form that we have been using so far, and that we first became acquainted with as the "Aeolian mode," is known as the *natural* form of the minor scale.

However, in practice, certain alternations of the natural form of the minor scale have been sanctioned by usage, the most frequent being to *raise* the seventh note of the scale a half tone. When this is done, we have the *harmonic* form of the minor scale. Here is what it would be in the key of E minor.

Still another form of the minor scale often met with is known as the *melodic* minor scale. In this case, both the sixth and seventh tone of the scale are *raised* a half tone, but only when the scale is ascending. On the way down we return to the natural form.

Here is the melodic form of the scale in E minor.

Notice the use of the natural sign (♮) to cancel the sharps previsously used on the same note. The three signs indicating sharps, flats, or naturals are called *accidentals,* and with a little practice you will learn to know them without having to think about them.

Now after this rather extended theoretical interlude, let us get back to music again. Here is the beginning of a very beautiful little piece by Robert Schumann, which should not be too difficult for you. It is called "First Loss," and, as you will see, uses the harmonic form of the key of E minor. It begins with the right hand in the higher octave, and we have written out the first few notes for you to help you get started.

Perhaps it may help you to learn the piece more easily if you practice those three measures in chord form, as well as the arpeggio form in which Schumann has written them.

They are the I, IV, and I chords in E minor, the very same chords that we learned in A minor.

Now let us go a little further with Schumann's piece, and try the first eight bars. As you will notice, the left hand starts in the G clef, and goes back to the bass clef as the range descends below middle C. As usual, it will help you at the beginning to work a little on each hand alone before putting them together.

Once you have learned the first eight bars, you have almost learned the first sixteen bars, for they are identical until the cadence in the last two bars. Up to now we have made liberal use of the repeat sign, and we might very well do it here too. But since this piece is by a great master, let us write it out exactly as he wrote it. Schumann has written out the repetition in full, and has used eighth notes rather than quarters. But the piece actually is not any faster in eighth notes than it was in quarter notes—it is simply a matter of choice for a composer's original sketches may happen to be different from his final version in this respect. But it is the character of the piece more than the choice of note values that determines the tempo. In this case, since the piece is quite clearly of a sad and reflective nature—the music itself would suggest this even without the title—our tempo will be rather on the slow side.*

If you can learn these sixteen bars, you have accomplished a great deal for this stage of the game, and you have learned some very beautiful music that you can play for your friends. Actually Schumann has extended this piece by adding a middle section, and then returning to the opening section which toward the end is interrupted by a few powerful chords.

We have printed the entire piece in the Musical Supplement at the end of the volume. By the time you have finished the book, you may be able to work out the entire piece. Perhaps as you continue working at the piano, you may wish to have the entire collection of Schumann's *Album for the Young* from which this selection is taken. There are many lovely pieces in it, and the ones at the beginning are not difficult at all.

*If you have a metronome set it to ♪=96. This does not mean that you will have to play the piece exactly metronomically in time—a very slight freedom of tempo is natural and inevitable in any musical performance—but at least the metronome can suggest a possible tempo, either the composer's or the editor's.

Suggestions for Practice

Again you may need quite a bit of time for this lesson—but don't go ahead until you feel that you know it thoroughly.

If you would like some extra practice in reading in new keys, get hold of the *Oxford Book for Older Beginners* (Oxford University Press). It is an excellent beginner's method, but somewhat more difficult than the Thompson book, for it begins immediately with a variety of keys, and introduces chords in the very first lesson.* It also offers a great deal of creative work for the student to try, and you will find it a most valuable addition to any other work you do.

*Don't be taken aback to find that the V7 chord as given in the Oxford book is different from the V7 chord that we have learned. This chord exists in a number of different positions, and the Oxford book has chosen a different one to begin with.

Counterpoint

So far all of the pieces we have learned have been based on the pattern of a melody harmonized with an accompaniment. But sometimes we will come across music that features two melodies of equal importance played simultaneously. This style of composition is called *contrapuntal* or *polyphonic*.

Let us experiment a little with *counterpoint*. It will help teach the hands to be independent, and it will serve as an introduction to a fascinating musical style.

There are certain musical forms that are particularly characteristic of the polyphonic style, and one of the simplest is the *canon* or *round*, in which one voice (if there are singers) or one instrument (if there are instruments) or one hand (if we are playing the piano) begins a melody, and a second voice or a second instrument, or the other hand, comes in with the same melody a little later, while the first voice continues it.

An excellent example of this musical form occurs in—yes, you guessed it "Frère Jacques," which we have already used as our first introduction to reading notes, and as our first exercise in changing keys.

Let us play "Frère Jacques" in the right hand without any harmonization, and this time we shall play it in the key of F Major, starting on the note F. The reason we have chosen the key of F is that it is the easiest key to sing it in, and if you happen to have a few friends around who would care to join in with you, it is possible to sing it in a round of as many as four voices. At the piano however, we shall content ourselves with just two voices, one for the right hand and one for the left.

Play it then in the right hand alone in our new key of F. This key has one flat, B-flat, which we shall put in the key signature at the beginning of the piece, and which we shall remember to play anytime we see a B in the music, which will now be a B-flat. As you will notice, the note B occurs in the third, fourth, fifth, and sixth measures, and if you'd like to remind yourself, you can pencil a flat in just before these notes.

Now play it in the left hand an octave lower.

Now we are ready to try it in canon form. Start the melody in the right hand, and at measure three the left hand will enter with the melody while the right hand continues. If you have ever sung "Frère Jacques" or any other simple round with friends—and who hasn't—this shouldn't offer any special difficulties. However, don't do it too fast at first, since those eighth notes aren't as easy as they look!

Perhaps you can think of other canons that you can sing or play. There are many folksongs that work in canon, and many composers have written canons for diversion, Purcell, Mozart, and Brahms among them.

Here is another simple canon that you can try, just for practice.

Moderato

Don't forget to play each hand alone before you put it together. Here is another little canon, in the minor mode this time. Again, play the hands alone first. The notation *sf* on the note D in the right hand in measure five and the left hand in measure six, is an abbreviation of the Italian word, *sforzando*, which means a strong accent.

Andante espressivo

As you continue to play the piano, you will find it fascinating to become acquainted with the vast wealth of contrapuntal music left by Johann Sebastian Bach (1685-1750) and other composers of his time. In another year or two you may be able to play some of Bach's *Inventions* for two voices, and later on you may get to know the wonderful fugues of *The Well-Tempered Clavier*. Fugues are a more elaborate contrapuntal form, and it may take some time before you can tackle them, but they will richly reward the study you put into them. Bach's *Well-Tempered Clavier* consists of two collections of twenty-four fugues in every one of the possible major and minor keys, each one preceded by a prelude.

Although these works of Bach are rather difficult technically, you will find before long that you can play his easier things, such as the teaching pieces that he wrote for his songs and for his second wife, Anna Magdalena Bach.

And if you would like to start some pieces in a contrapuntal style right now, you might look up the *Mikrokosmos* by the Hungarian composer Béla Bartók, one of the most gifted of twentieth-century composers. They are written in a rather more unconventional musical idiom than we have used so far, but they are intended for the earliest beginners at the piano, and you may find it an interesting challenge to see what you can do with these pieces. The first of the six volumes that comprise this collection should not be beyond your abilities at the present time.

Suggestions for Practice

If you would like to vary the canons in this lesson, try reversing the hands. In "Frère Jacques," for example, start the melody in the left hand, and then come in at measure three with the melody in the right hand. You can do this with all the canons we have had, but you may find it necessary to write them out yourself the new way before playing them.

And along with your exercises, and the pieces you review, choose a few selections from Bartók's *Mikrokosmos* to read and to learn. Some of them are canonic in form, and they will give you additional practice in a polyphonic style.

A Prelude by Bach—1

In our earlier chapters we have discussed harmony chiefly as a means of accompanying the melodies we have learned. But sometimes changing harmonies are so beautiful in themselves that they can form the basis for a piece of music. One such example is the prelude to the first fugue of Bach's *Well-Tempered Clavier*.

We spoke of *The Well-Tempered Clavier* in the last chapter as a work of such difficulty that you could hardly expect to tackle it for a number of years. That is true of the fugues that make up this collection—but some of the preludes are much easier than the fugues they introduce, and the first prelude presents so few problems technically that you may even be able to start playing it right now.

Actually, this piece consists of a series of chords played one after another in a simple arpeggio pattern.

Here is the chord of the first measure.

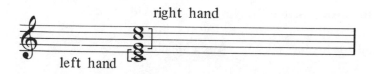

It is a C Major chord going up from middle C with two notes repeated in the higher octave. Divide it between the hands so that the left hand plays the two lowest notes (middle C and the E above), while the right hand plays the remaining three notes (G, C above, and E above).

Now play the chord quite slowly and softly as an arpeggio, with the left hand still taking the two lowest notes, and the right hand the other three.

Now do this again, but let the right hand repeat the three notes, as follows.

This time we have written it on two staves, and included Bach's indication that the two left-hand notes be sustained. You can also keep the notes of the right hand held down too, if you wish, since this is entirely in keeping with the style of the piece.

As you play this arpeggio very softly, listen carefully to the sound of the
C Major chord. With a sensitive and delicate touch, even a simple C Major
chord can be a thing of beauty! As a matter of fact, Bach liked it so much
that he asks us to play the entire arpeggio pattern twice, as follows. (You may
use any fingering that is comfortable for you, but the fingering given below
should be natural for most hands.)

Now we are ready for the next chord. Keep the middle C in the third finger of the left hand, while changing the E to a D. In the right hand, the entire
chord moves up a note. Here are the two opening chords of the piece.

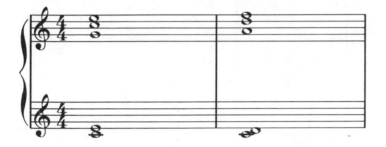

Can you play this new chord in the same arpeggio pattern we used in the
opening C Major chord? Here it is written out.

In the next chord, we take the lowest tone in each hand down one note.
Play it with the two opening chords that you have just learned.

Once you learn this new chord, it's perfectly easy to put it into the same arpeggio pattern we used for the other chords. Here it is written out.

After that we return to the C Major chord just as we had it at first. This gives us the first four chords of Bach's prelude. Get to know them well in their chord forms, as follows.

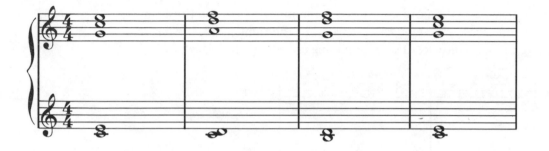

And then practice them in the arpeggio forms that Bach uses in this prelude.

If you can do these four chords, there is no reason why you can't go further. Here is the first phrase of Bach's C Major prelude, written in chord form.

The seven chords that follow the first four that we have learned are a little more difficult in some ways, for the right hand will have to stretch an octave in bars five and seven, and Bach has introduced some F-sharps that lead us from the key of C to the key of G. But learn these new chords very carefully one by one, and it will be only a matter of time before you can play the entire section.

Perhaps you may find that you can learn these chords more easily in the arpeggio form that Bach has used. Here is the passage written out that way. This time though, we shall write it in eighth notes rather than quarter notes —it may be easier to grasp the flow of the piece in this notation. But it doesn't have to be any faster than it was when you read it in quarter notes.

Remember to keep the soft and delicate quality throughout, holding
down all the notes of the chord as long as possible.

Once you have gotten this far with the Bach prelude, you have accomplished a great deal, and you can rest for a little while on your laurels!

The Pedals

Of course you've noticed the pedals on your piano, and if you've resisted the temptation to fool around with them a little, then you have a lot of will power! But they are most important, and we might as well learn something about them.

Pianos have either two or three pedals, and if your piano has three pedals the middle one may not work (it doesn't on many pianos), and even if it does you won't need it for a long time.

The one on the left is the "soft pedal," which reduces the sound of the piano by moving the hammers or the strings slightly. You won't need this for quite a while either.

But the pedal on the right is extremely important. Commonly known as the "loud pedal" in contrast to the soft pedal, it is really a *sustaining* pedal. If you press it down, it will allow any note that is played to continue sounding until you let it up again.

If you will go back to the first measure of the Bach prelude and this time play it while keeping the pedal down, you will find that it acquires a new and beautiful resonance. In case you like the sound of the pedal you may think of playing the piece as far as you have gone with the pedal down throughout.

However, it's not quite as easy as it seems when you only do one measure alone. If you were to keep the pedal down throughout, the different chords would run into each other and begin to sound muddy. You have to change the pedal when the chords change—but it won't do either just to change the pedal as you change the fingers for the new chord; that would allow a break in the sound between the chords that would be crude and unartistic.

The pedal does have to change every time the chord changes, but there is a little trick of coordination involved that is quite essential in connecting chords with the pedal, and we might as well learn now.

Let us take the first four chords of the Bach prelude in chord form for practice. Review them first without pedal.

The opening chord is no problem, for you can simply put the right foot down on the pedal as you play the chord. But when you change to the next chord, your foot must go *up* just as your fingers go down on the new chord, and only then, after your foot has gone up, can it go down again as you continue to hold the chord.

Perhaps this may be easier to learn at first if you try it with only one hand at a time. Let us try the first two chords in the right hand only, and see if we can get this trick of coordination. And perhaps we can break it down into still smaller steps.

Start the first chord in the right hand again as you put the pedal down—no problem there! It's only when you change the chord that you have to concentrate. Now as you keep holding the right hand and the foot down, think of the next step you have to do, which will be to raise the hand for the next chord while you continue to hold the foot down. Let's do that and call it Step One—it's not particularly hard by itself.

Now while you keep the position you've just reached—hand up and foot down—prepare for Step Two, which is where the trick of coordination really comes in. Now you must simultaneously raise the foot just as you put the hand down on the new chord. (Do that now, and remember that the foot must go up just at the precise moment that the hand comes down.)

Now you are ready for Step Three, which is very simple. Having lowered the hand on the new chord while raising the foot, keep the hand down while you bring the foot down again too. That's not very hard by itself, either.

Very well then, let us review these three steps to make quite sure that we have them straight. Do them as slowly as you want, so that you know just where you are.

First, of course, play the opening chord as you put the pedal down. Then:

Step One — raise the hand for the new chord while keeping the foot down.

Step Two — lower the hand on the new chord while simultaneously raising the foot.

Step Three— keep holding the new chord and put the foot down again.

Well, if you've gotten that—and give yourself a while for it, since it can be a little tricky at first—then let's extend it by going ahead with the following chords in the right hand.

Between chords two and three, do *exactly* what you did between chords one and two. Go back over the steps and read them carefully while you do it. Then follow the same steps from chord three to chord four.

When you begin to feel that you have it, then you can go over the whole series of the four chords, this time with both hands together. You will find that you can master it if you only have a little patience.

There are a few different ways of writing in the pedaling that indicates the process quite graphically. Here first is the old fashioned way that was in use during the nineteenth century. The abbreviation *"Ped"* in the old Gothic script under a note indicates that you put the pedal down, and an asterisk (*) indicates that you release it. Here are our four chords with this notation.

A more modern notation is a line underneath the music, lowered when the pedal goes down and raised when it goes up. Here are our four chords with this notation.

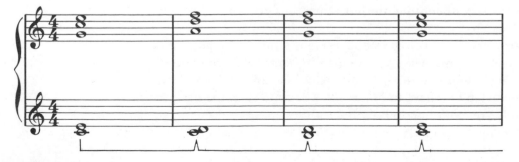

Most often, though, the pedal is simply left to the pianist's discretion, and a direction *"con Pedale"* is given as a general indication that the pedal is to be used. Indeed, the pedal is used so much as a matter of course that it is perfectly legitimate to use it where you think it would be appropriate, even when there is no indication of any kind in the music. Different pianists use the pedal to different degrees, and it is used more frequently in certain styles of music than in others.

Generally speaking, the pedal is not used in polyphonic music, or where the motion of the music is largely stepwise. But where there are arpeggios, or where slow chords have to be connected, or where the harmonic underpinning is important, then the pedal can be used freely at your own discretion. You should listen very carefully to your pedaling. Don't allow it to become careless, or use it to cover up shoddy finger work. Each pianist learns to feel the pedal in his own way, and as you keep using it and learning about it, it will eventually get to be second nature to you.

Suggestions for Practice

You might like to go back over some of your old pieces now, and see which ones might profit from a little use of the pedal. Perhaps you might try the pedal with the waltz we had in the lesson on Rests. Play this piece again, and hold the pedal down on the last two measures. Or if you'd like to experiment with a greater use of the pedal, try it this way, changing the pedal at every bar.

Try the chords in Robert Schumann's delightful "Choral" from *Album for the Young*. Use the pedal throughout, changing it at every chord, as we have learned in this chapter. It makes an excellent pedal exercise.

The pedal can also be used in "A Short Study" from the same *Album*. It is actually an arpeggio prelude, somewhat comparable to the prelude by Bach that we have been working on. Use the pedal for each measure, and change it, with a quick up and down motion of the foot, just as you play the first note of each new measure. For your pleasure, we have included both pieces in the Musical Supplement.

A Prelude by Bach—2

A piece like the Bach C Major prelude naturally calls for a continuous use of the pedal, even though it may not be marked in the music. Indeed, this piece was not written for the piano, but for the predecessors of the piano, the harpsichord or the clavichord, which had no pedals at all. These instruments had no damper mechanism either, to stop the sounds of the notes as they were let go, and so they automatically continued to sound, although at a much lower level of volume than in our modern pianos.

This little prelude by Bach, then, should be played with the pedal in constant use, being changed carefully at every change of the chord. When the piece is played in the arpeggio form in which it is written, the entire process of changing the pedal takes place on the first note of the arpeggio of the new chord, and you will have to learn to change the pedal easily and quickly enough so that it will not take more than the time of a single short note. Actually, the two steps of lifting the pedal and then putting it down again as you change the chord, can be done so closely together that they become almost a single step.

Here are the first few measures of Bach's prelude as he wrote them, with the pedal changes indicated in modern notation. In the last chapter we saw the prelude written in both quarter notes and eighth notes, but Bach himself actually used sixteenth notes, and we shall use them here too. There are two sixteenth notes to an eighth note, or four sixteenth notes to a quarter note.

sixteenth notes:

♪ ♪ ♪ ♪ or ♫♫

sixteenth rest: ♩

In a passage that is written in sixteenth notes throughout, you can establish your tempo in terms of the sixteenth notes, and you don't actually have to play the sixteenth notes any faster than you played the quarter notes in the last chapter.

You might find it interesting to listen to different recordings of this prelude. It has been recorded by many great pianists, and some performers have played it on Bach's own instrument, the harpsichord. Wanda Landowska is the musician who has revived the use of the harpsichord in modern times, and her performance is a fascinating thing, for she has made an artistic creation of great beauty and power out of this little prelude.

In some manuscripts of this piece, Bach has written only the first few measures in arpeggio form, and has indicated the rest of the piece simply by writing the chords. Obviously, if each chord follows an identical arpeggio pattern, it is not too hard to figure it out from the chords alone. If you are interested in the continuation of the piece, here are the chords of the eight-bar phrase that follows the first eleven bars that we had in the previous chapter.

If you were able to learn the first phrase that we worked on in the last chapter, then you can learn the whole piece, and we have printed it in its entirety in the Musical Supplement. If you like it, try to learn it all. It will richly reward any time you can put into it, for Bach's music has a marvelous grandeur and serenity that comes through even in this little prelude.

Suggestions for Practice

Although Bach's prelude presents no serious difficulties from the point of view of finger technique, you will have to plan to leave a good deal of time to learn it, and particularly to memorize it, for it is rather an extended composition, and each of the five-note chords must be learned very carefully.

Divide it into sections, and learn each section separately, almost as though it were a piece in itself. We took the first eleven bars as one section, and we have continued with another section of eight bars. The next four bars begin a new section leading to an eight-bar phrase on a "pedal point" (that is to say, these eight bars all have the same bass note, G, over which the chords are built). Learn these twelve bars as another section—dividing it if you wish, into two smaller sections of four and eight bars. Then the rest of the piece can make another section for you to learn.

Of course you will have to keep each of these sections sufficiently in practice once you have learned them to be able to put them together eventually to form the entire prelude. Even a period of a few months is not too much to allow yourself to learn this piece. And once you have learned it, don't lose it! Make a point of reviewing it every so often to be sure that it remains in your fingers.

If you would like to play more Bach, you might like to look into his collection of *Twelve Little Preludes*. The third of these twelve preludes is an arpeggio prelude in C minor that you should be able to master. Some of the other preludes in the set of twelve may not be too difficult for you; the second is another good one to work on. Practice it at first like an exercise, with very strongly articulated finger action, and later on see if you can make it sound interesting as a piece of music.

Some Czerny

We have been going ahead so fast with such a variety of new material that you may have been tempted to neglect our old technical exercises. But don't! They are important, all of them, spending a little time at each of your practice sessions with one or another of them, including even the very first five-finger exercises. Practice the scales as exercises too—they are very valuable in this way, for they provide practice in crossing the thumb under, which is a technique that you always have to make use of.

We are coming to the end of our little book now, but before we close, let us advance another step with our exercises and try something more difficult. Here is a passage in "thirds"; that is to say, notes that are three steps apart. You will find that this is more difficult than playing a single note at a time, but practice it slowly and carefully and you will get it.

Now try the same thing an octave lower in the left hand.

And now both hands together.

This is a most useful kind of practice; do it very strongly and slowly, always articulating very distinctly.

If you would like a little variety in this exercise, try it in the following canonic version.

(left hand)

We have called our chapter "Some Czerny" and if you are wondering about Czerny, he was a composer who had a special genius for inventing finger exercises.* He wrote enormous quantities of them, and they all very ingeniously manage to find some special way to help develop your technical capacity.

The foregoing exercise in thirds is a good preparation for this piece by Czerny, which makes something a little more musical out of this technical problem. See if you can learn it. It is not too easy, but it is well worth working on, and with practice you will find that you can get it.

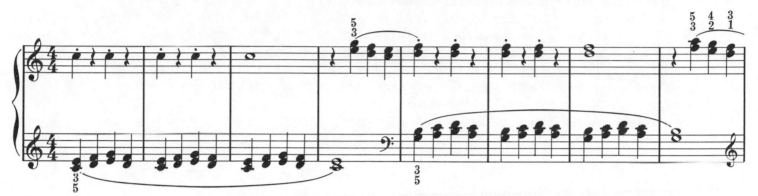

(Between measures eight and nine, you can't make the passage in thirds completely *legato* in the right hand, but hold the thumb while you cross the second and fourth fingers over it.)

Here is the beginning of another clever study by Czerny.

As you notice, it begins like a five-finger exercise, but turns on itself to give the weaker fingers additional practice.

*Carl Czerny was the teacher of Franz Liszt, who is regarded as the greatest pianist of all time, and perhaps it is only fair to attribute Liszt's achievement in some degree to Czerny's gifts as a teacher as well as to Liszt's own brilliant genius. Czerny was also one of Beethoven's pupils, and is thus a link between two of the great giants of musical history. Czerny brought Liszt as a child prodigy to meet Beethoven, who, although almost deaf in his later years and very touchy and hard to please, was so impressed by the boy that he kissed him on the forehead and told him: "You are very fortunate, for you will bring joy to many people." Liszt has a moving account of this incident which, although it occured when he was only twelve, he always thought of as the high point of his musical career.

After this passage is repeated, Czerny then switches to an arpeggio figure as follows.

Practice it carefully, for it's not quite as easy as it looks. Czerny repeats this too, and then finishes with the following scale.

Epilogue

One of the most valuable things you can derive from working at the piano—even if you never get to be an expert performer—is a heightened awareness of the skill and beauty of other pianists' playing. You can attend a piano recital now and appreciate it in a way that you never could have if you hadn't learned a little about playing the piano yourself. Actually, a recital by a great pianist can be among the memorable experiences of your life, and you should take the opportunity of hearing good pianists whenever you can.

And if there are reviews of the concerts you hear, you might find it interesting to compare your reactions with those of the critics. Don't be afraid to stand up for your own opinions, though, even if you disagree with the critics; they often disagree among themselves anyway. But a good review is often worth reading for itself. Some of the outstanding critics of recent times have had their reviews collected in book form. The composer Virgil Thomson, who worked on the New York *Herald Tribune* for a number of years, is an interesting one to look into. And in London, just before the turn of the century, George Bernard Shaw was a music critic for a while before he began writing plays. Being a great writer as well as a music lover of acute perception, his reviews are just as interesting to read now as when they were written. They have been collected into four volumes, and there is hardly a dull page among them. Among the great composers, Schumann, Berlioz, and Debussy were all remarkable critics whose reviews brilliantly recreate the musical life of their time.

You may also find it stimulating to read some of the books devoted to the great pianists of our time and of former times. Abram Chasins' *Speaking of Pianists* describes his own personal friendships with many of the great pianists of our day, and is filled with interesting ideas and suggestions about playing the piano that you can often make use of yourself. Harold Schonberg's *The Great Pianists* weaves a fascinating tapestry of pianistic history in which all the great names come to life.

By all accounts, Franz Liszt was the greatest pianist of all time, and even in his own day he became a legend. Here is an account by Robert Schumann of one occasion:

> First he played with the public as if to try it, then gave it something more profound, until he enmeshed every member of the audience with his art and did with them as he willed. With the exception of Paganini, no artist to a like degree possesses this power of subjecting the public, or lifting it, sustaining it, and letting it fall again. . . .Within a few seconds tenderness, boldness, exquisiteness, wildness succeed one another; the instrument glows and flashes under the master's hands. . . .But he must be heard—and also seen; for if Liszt played behind a screen, a great deal of poetry would be lost.

And here is how he appeared to the French composer Camille Saint-Saëns, on another occasion:

> I had already considered him to be a genius and had formed in advance an almost impossible conception of his pianism. Judge of my astonishment when I realized that he far exceeded even this expectation. The dreams of my youthful fancy were but prose beside the Dionysiac poetry evoked by his supernatural fingers. . . .As I write I see again that long pale face casting seductive glances at his audience while from beneath his

fingers, almost unconsciously, and with an amazing range of nuance, there murmured, surged, boomed and stormed the waves of the *Legende de St. François marchant sur les Flots.* Never again shall we hear or see anything like it.

The only pianist since Liszt's time who has been even compared to him is the great Anton Rubinstein, who made his impression on Saint-Saëns:

> With his irresistible charm and superhuman playing, Rubinstein could stand up fearlessly to the memory of Liszt. He was very different from him of course, and if Liszt was an eagle, then Rubinstein was a lion. Those who have heard him play can never forget the sight of that great sheathed claw of his stroking the keyboard with its powerful caress! Neither one nor the other was ever at any moment the "pianist." Even when they played the smallest things very simply, they remained great, without deliberation and through the grandeur of complete integrity. They were living incarnations of their art and worked miracles, imposing a sort of holy terror beyond the limit of ordinary admiration. As often as he wished, and with no other resource than himself and a piano, we have seen Rubinstein pack the enormous Theatre de l'Eden with quivering multitudes and fill it with such resounding and gradated vibrations as might have been those of an orchestra. And when he joined forces with the orchestra itself, what an astonishing role was played by the instrument at his fingers across that ocean of sonority! You can get an idea of it by imagining a flash of lightning through a strong cloud. How he made the piano sing! What magic did he possess to give those velvety sounds a lingering duration which they did not have, cannot have, under the fingers of any other?

And yet Rubinstein himself is said to have declared, "Compared to Liszt, we are all children!"

It is tantalizing to spectulate as to whether any of the pianists of our time are comparable to the giants of the past. By now it is a little hard to know how much of their greatness is legend and how much reality. Perhaps indeed, the legend may have grown because their playing was never taken down on records to be studied and scrutinized. In our time, at least, all the great pianists have been recorded, and we can listen to them in the quiet of our own homes as well as in the midst of the excitement of the concert stage.

Of course there have been many superb pianists since the time of Liszt and Rubinstein. In the early years of this century Ignacy Paderewski is said to have aroused much of the same type of audience hysteria that they did. Although the few records we possess of Paderewski were made at the end of his career when his powers were on the decline, it is still possible to sense something of his greatness in them. And in recent years—although they are no longer with us—we have had some wonderful recordings by Arthur Schnabel in the classical repertory of Beethoven and Schubert, and some perfect gems of style and elegance by the gifted Rumanian pianist, Dinu Lipatti, who died at the age of thirty-three. And we should not forget our own Artur Rubinstein. Or the brilliant Vladimir Horowitz. Or the magesterial Sviatoslav Richter. Or scores of others.

Go to as many concerts as you can, listen to as many records as you can, and learn what you can from pianists who are better than you. But always remember that there is no substitute for the joy of making music yourself.

If you have mastered this book on your own, you have accomplished a great deal, even though you have only just begun to scratch the surface! By now, if you have not already found one, you must look for a teacher who is well qualified and sympathetic to you. As you continue to work and improve, you will find that the pleasure that music can bring to you is limitless.

Bibliography

Music

Denes Agay, *The Young Pianist's First Book* (Warner Bros. Music)
Excellent material to supplement our first lesson in sight reading.

John Thompson, *The Book for Older Beginners* (Willis Music Co.)

John Thompson, *The Oxford Book for Older Beginners* (Oxford University Press)
These are two of the finest beginner's methods for older pupils, and are quite different in approach. Both of them are well worth having.

Styron and Stevens, *Start Pedalling* (Summy-Birchard Co.)
Introduces all aspects of pedalling at a beginning level.

Denes Agay, *The Joy of Bach* (Yorktown Music Press)
Original keyboard pieces by members of the Bach family.

Robert Schumann, *Album for the Young*
A set of 45 pieces for beginners by the great romantic master. Not all of these are easy, but the entire collection should be in your library.

Béla Bartók, *Mikrokosmos*
A collection somewhat similar to Schumann's by the twentieth century Hungarian composer. There are six volumes in all, and the first two should be within your range after you have finished this book.

Denes Agay, *Easy Classics to Moderns* (Consolidated Music Publishers)
A great variety of material to supplement the work we have done.

Books

Howard Shanet, *Learn to Read Music* (Simon and Schuster)
If you are serious about learning how to read music, this book will be most helpful.

Murphy and Stringham, *Creative Harmony and Musicianship* (Prentice-Hall)
A splendid introduction to creative work, which really begins at the beginning.

Charles Cooke, *Playing the Piano for Pleasure* (Simon and Schuster)
A delightful and stimulating book, filled with good advice.

Harold Schönberg, *The Great Pianists* (Simon and Schuster)

Abram Chasins, *Speaking of Pianists* (Alfred A. Knopf)
These two books offer fascinating background about the great pianists of the past and of our time, and provide many incidental hints about playing the piano.

Arthur Loesser, *Men, Women & Pianos* (Simon and Schuster)
This book is filled with fascinating lore about the origin and development of the piano, and its place in society through the centuries.

Albert Einstein, *A Short History of Music* (Alfred A. Knopf)

Harvard Brief Dictionary of Music (Harvard University Press)

Musical Supplement

Three Studies

    We have printed this study as Czerny wrote it, with chords in the left hand. It is followed by a variation in which the exercise is given to the left hand and the chords to the right. When you have learned these two studies practice them in different ways—sometimes loud and sometimes soft; sometimes *legato* and sometimes *staccato*; sometimes slow and sometimes fast. They are so valuable that you can use them as standbys long after you have gone on to other things, much as you did with the very first five-finger exercises.

Carl Czerny

*This symbol **C** is a commonly used abbreviation of $\frac{4}{4}$ time.

III

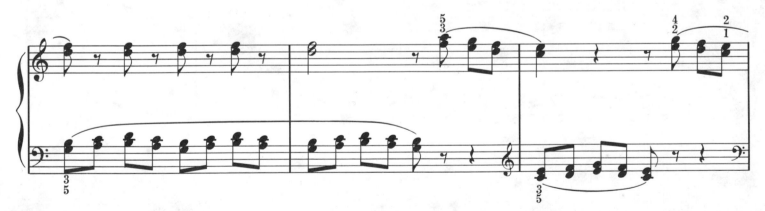

Album for the Young

These next three pieces are from Schumann's *Album for the Young*.

Here is "First Loss" in its entirety. The middle section and the ending are more difficult than the first sixteen bars which we learned earlier. Work on them a bar or two at a time with the hands alone at first, and then put them together slowly, increasing the tempo little by little as you practice it. The powerful chords in the fourth bar before the end you may imagine, if you wish, as a musical interpretation of a child's sobbing.

Schumann has indicated the tempo as *Nicht schnell* (not fast) which allows a considerable leeway. You may play it first slowly as ♪=96 and later, if you like, bring it up to ♩=72.

First Loss

Robert Schumann

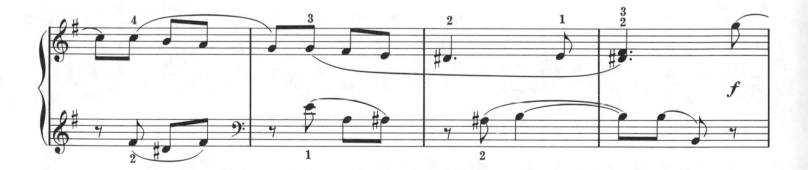

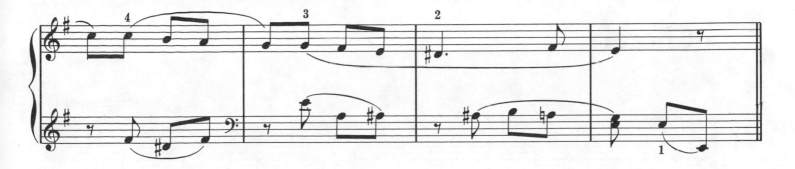

(somewhat slower)

cresc.

a Tempo

f

f   f   p

Chorale

Robert Schumann

(Freue dich, o meine Seele) ♩=54

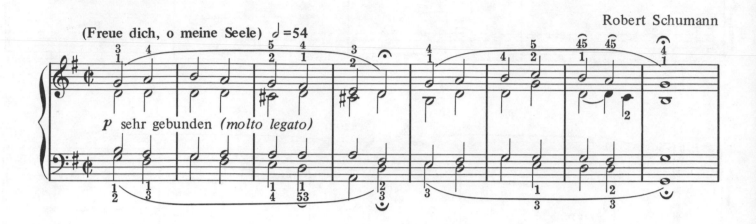

p sehr gebunden (molto legato)

mf

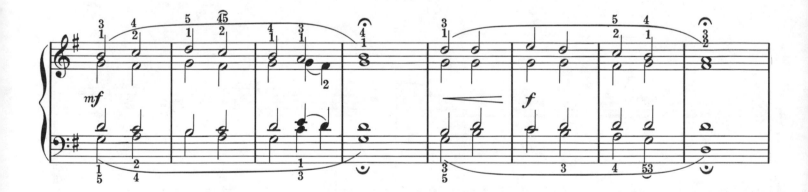

A Short Study

Robert Schunmann

Leise und sehr egal zu spielen

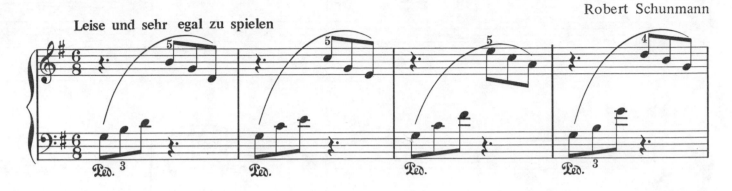

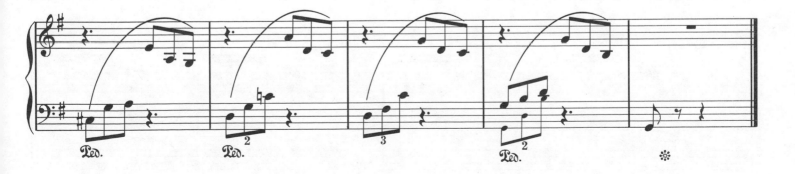

Prelude in C Major

We have discussed this beautiful piece from Book I of *The Well-Tempered Clavier* at length. After you can play the passages we have studied before, see if you can learn the entire piece as given below.

Johann Sebastian Bach

Seven Pieces on Five Notes

Here are two pieces from Igor Stravinsky's inventive collection of five-finger compositions.

Andantino

Igor Stravinsky

Da Capo al Fine

Lento

Igor Stravinsky

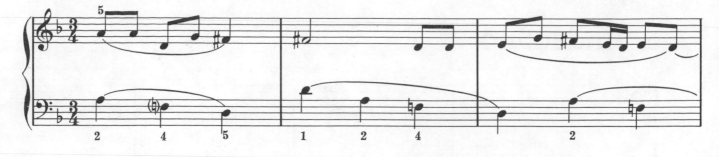